MY FAITH JOURNEY

BONIFACE DAAWIEH-KEELSON

PUBLISHED 2021 BY DAAWIEHBOOKS AND DREAMHAUZ
PUBLICATIONS
Cover Design & Interior Layout / Formatting by: Quest Publications
Email: *questpublications@outlook.com*

FOR ADDITIONAL INFORMATION WRITE TO:
Boniface Daawieh-Keelson
DarwiehBooks and Publications
P.O. Box AF 657, Adenta-Accra,
Ghana, West Africa

OR Contact me on the following Cell Phones
001-233 244765586
001-233 244684802

My other contacts are Email:
amawaa@yahoo.com
evangelistboniface@ymail.com
bonifacekeelson@gmail.com

Social Media:
www.facebook.com/boniface.keelson
www.facebook.com/boniface.keelson

ISBN: 978-1-988439-28-0

TABLE OF CONTENT

THE JOURNEY

INTRODUCTION

My Faith Journey chronicles my walk with God from my childhood up to the attainment of my golden jubilee (50 years). The focus of the book is purely on my walk with God and not my life in general.

I got born again on February 19, 1984 whilst in secondary school form one. This was when a GHAFES (Ghana Fellowship of Evangelical Students) brother I would simply refer to as FAY, came from the University of Science and Technology to preach in our school. In response to an altar call for those who wished to be born again, I gave my life to the Lord.

Prior to this landmark incident, I had always been interested in the things of God and had even read the

Bible from cover to cover about three times before entering secondary school.

In my childhood days, when I was 6 years old, I remember taking on the role of a pastor over a group of fellow young children as we held church services in an uncompleted building in the compound where we lived. I would always stand in front of my friends and playmates to conduct services, where I preached to them.

Unfortunately, till date, I am unable to remember a single sermon I preached in those days.

Whilst in primary school, my Dad insisted I became a Mass Server in the Catholic church where we attended church at the time. I served joyfully as a Mass Server and was the darling boy of all the priests till I entered secondary school.

I had always longed to know God better and have a closer personal walk with Him.

My born-again experience therefore gave me an opportunity to begin a sincere walk with the Lord all through my secondary school days till date.

When I was about turning 50, I thought of jotting down how far I had come in my Christian Journey in appreciation and thanksgiving to the Lord. These Christian landmarks are what I have chronicled in simplified blocks in this book for quicker and easier reading.

I trust it may inspire you.

God Bless You!

BONIFACE

1

BORN AGAIN

BORN AGAIN IN FORM ONE

I got born again through the preaching of a GHAFES brother, brother Fay, from Independence Hall – UST (University of Science and Technology). The day was Sunday, and the date was February 19, 1984 at a school protestant church service. I was in secondary school form one. Brother Fay became my first spiritual father and I visited him in his hall of residence several times. Unfortunately, I lost touch with him because I left Kumasi to continue my secondary education in Koforidua just after form one. In those days, communication was not as easy as it is today. I have since not been able to trace him because I did not know his proper name at the time save his initials by which he was affectionately called—FAY. God richly bless him wherever he is for coming to preach to us and leading me to personal salvation.

2

POPE JOHN DAYS

BAPTISED IN THE HOLY GHOST IN 1985

At the end of my form one academic year—
1983/1984, in Kumasi, my uncle who was a
lecturer at UST (University of Science and
Technology) moved me from Kumasi to Pope John
Secondary School in Koforidua. This was to enable
his bosom friend at the time, the then headmaster of
the school, Rev. Father Nomo to keep an eye on me.
He felt I was taking the born-again 'stuff' too far and
needed to be at a place far from all the S.U. (Scripture
Union) and fellowship engagements. I am glad he
took that decision because it helped me to focus on
my schooling, however, it did not quench my fire in
the Lord at all. Little did my dear uncle know that

there was S.U. at Pope John Secondary School as well. I immediately joined the S.U. group in my new school. I developed the art of praying alone during lunch hours in the school chapel. I used almost all my lunch hours for personal prayers and bible studies and only attended lunch when there was a threat to punish those who absented themselves.

On Tuesday, March 19, 1985, during my usual school lunch hour prayers in the school chapel, I received the Holy Ghost Baptism whilst praying alone. I began to speak in the spirit (in tongues) for the first time. It was a great experience.

SPIRITUAL LEADERSHIP @ POPE JOHN

I became so active in the Scripture Union that my commitment could be attested to by everyone including those who were not members. I was put on programs and asked to lead prayer sessions by the leadership. It therefore did not come as a surprise when I was appointed the Assistant Prayer Secretary of the Scripture Union Group during my 3rd term in form 2 to my 3rd term in form 3.

When the Prayer Secretary who was a sixth former was about to complete school, he recommended that I be appointed as the prayer secretary of the fellowship. So, from my 3rd term in form 3 to my 3rd term in form 5 I served as the prayer secretary of the fellowship at Pope John Secondary School.

INITIATIVES ON POPE JOHN CAMPUS

I used my spiritual influence and my position of leadership to initiate the following moves whilst a student on Pope John Secondary School Campus:

I mobilized a group of students to fast and pray twice a week, and sometimes more. Some junior seminarians who had become born again and left the junior seminary into the mainstream school also joined my group. [NOTE: Pope John Secondary School had a Junior Seminary wing for those who intended to go to major seminaries after secondary school and turn out as Reverend Fathers in future. Though, we all attended classes in the same classrooms, they had their own block separated from the mainstream and received extra spiritual classes and exercises which were peculiar to them alone]. Since some of the boys who left the seminary for the mainstream joined my group, it was commonly reported that I was the one indoctrinating some of the seminarians to leave the seminary and embrace what was referred to as 'all this born-again nonsense.' I was summoned before the Reverend Father who was the school chaplain to explain myself and I was seriously cautioned. From that time, all my movements were strictly monitored with some students being set as spies on me. I was called to the headmaster's office a few times and I was eventually reported to my uncle. But for my uncle's relationship with the headmaster, and the fact that I was brilliant and liked by most of my teachers, I would have been dealt with seriously by the school. Interestingly, the school chaplain decided to attend our S. U. services to witness personally what we preached to the students. For almost all the times he attended our services, it was either a patron who was a tutor or me preaching. He felt deeply in love with my preaching and looked forward to being at fellowship anytime I was preaching. He quoted me a few times at the general school assembly and even used some of the bible texts I used to preach to address the entire school. Looking back today, I can testify that, almost all the students who were in my prayer and fasting group at the time, are currently active in ministry as church elders or pastors. Glory be to God!

Together with one sixth former (Edward Asabre), we formed a fellowship at the school kitchen. Every Sunday after breakfast we would go to the school kitchen and hold a one-hour church service with the kitchen staff, since they were unable to go to church because of us. We talked to the Reverend Father who was the school chaplain as well as the headmaster about it and we were given the green light to do this. Every Sunday morning, we had wonderful services with the kitchen staff. Initially, it was only the two of us, but shortly we had a team of 5 boys going with us every Sunday morning. Recently I received a text message from one of the boys who joined us in the kitchen ministry which reads:

> More grace Sir,
>
> You have never ceased to inspire me since our kitchen evangelism days back at Pope John Secondary School.
>
> God richly bless you!
> Adam Rahman

Unfortunately, the sixth former and I both left Pope John the same year (1989). We entrusted the 'Pantry Church Service' into the hands of the others we recruited but we never followed up to see how the ministry to our dear kitchen staff was sustained.

My third and last initiative in Pope John was to go to St. Joseph Hospital on every other Sunday afternoon to share the word of God with those hospitalized and to also pray with them. I got a few of the S.U. brothers to join me in this ministry. The hospital shares a boundary with the school and so we only had to walk through the school farm into the hospital. It was a delightful and very fulfilling ministry during my school days at Pope John.

3

OPOKU WARE DAYS

BACK TO KUMASI FOR SIXTH FORM

I was in secondary school form five in 1988/89 academic year. I sat for my Ordinary Level Certificate Exam (O' Level) towards the end of the academic year. In selecting a sixth form school whilst registering for the exam, I chose Opoku Ware School without a word to either my Dad or my uncle. When the results came, I had passed very well and I therefore found my way back to Kumasi in the 1989/90 academic year.

BAPTIZED IN WATER IN OSOFO AMOAKO'S MINISTRY IN 1990

Our school—the Opoku Ware school was not far from the Evangelist Francis Akwasi Amoako's fellowship grounds. So, I made my way to the fellowship every Saturday morning without an exeat. Most students strolled to that part of the community to buy one or two things, so it was normal to go that far without an exeat even though it was still not officially allowed. At the fellowship, I endeared myself to Rev. Kusi Berko, Rev. Elvis Bediako (now Bishop Asare Bediako), Rev. John Olu (Rev. Elvis' friend who visited sometimes), Rev. Odaanor, Rev. Atuahene, Rev. Yaw Adu, Rev. Gyamfi, Rev. Abonuakese and even Osofo Akwasi Amoako.

I joined the class that was being prepared for baptism by immersion. On May 12, 1990, I was baptised by immersion along with others by some of the Resurrection Power Ministers in a river by the Santasi Roundabout.

SPIRITUAL IMPACT AT OPOKU WARE

Beside attending Rev. Amoako's fellowship on Saturdays, I was also actively involved in the S.U. as well as the protestant church on the school campus. Towards the end of the academic year in my lower sixth form, I was appointed the prayer secretary of the S.U. I took over from Senior Sammy Jones (currently a seasoned pastor in London).

I led the group on a series of fasting and prayers. I called for a few dawn prayers at the sixth form block, one of which landed us in serious trouble with the headmaster – Mr. Dapaa Berko. He asked all of us to go home because he caught us praying around 5am in the classroom. Filled with the boldness of the Lord, I led a few brothers to his house to plead with him. (No student dared to go to his house in those days). By the intervention of God, I obtained favour from him and he liked and appreciated my boldness. Not only did he rescind his decision to send us packing but would wave at me anytime he saw me after that incident.

I played a vital role in the protestant church services and was given the platform to preach on few occasions. Unfortunately, the chaplain – Rev. Father Luke had several misgivings about the protestant service and even called for its suspension for a while, few months to completing my sixth form.

Whilst on Opoku Ware campus, I preached some "Hell" sermons in the SU meetings and among some of my fellow sixth formers which led to the true conversion of some of the students including my mates. A few of them are into ministry as full time or part-time pastors today.

4

A'LEVEL NATIONAL SERVICE

LIFE IN KUMASI AFTER OPOKU WARE

After my sixth form education, I stayed in Kumasi for a while going on some ministry rounds with the late Rev. Kusi Berko. It was during this time that I wrote a beautiful poem on Jesus which I used to share on various platforms. The poem was also recorded on tape and captioned DIVINE ADORATION. Even though the poem was originally in English, Rev Kusi Berko decided to translate it into Twi at the studio. As a result of this, one side of the tape had the poem in Twi whilst the other side was in English.

NATIONAL SERVICE AFTER SIXTH FORM

The practice in those days was to offer a one-year national service after your sixth form education before continuing with your education. Few weeks to our national service postings, I left Kumasi and went to be with my parents at Akwatia. When the postings were published, I was posted to a small farming village between Akim Oda and New Abirem known as Breku. Vehicles did not ply the route to that village in those days. One had to get to the closest village where the vehicles stopped and walk about 5 miles to the village.

At the village I was put in a small room (mud house) as the accommodation offered me by the village chief. I enjoyed my stay with the people and mingled with them easily.

There was a small Pentecostal church – (the only church) in the village so I immediately joined to fellowship with them. I assisted the presiding elder greatly and became almost the pastor of the church. I had a great impact on the church and the community.

When the national service period was over and I had to leave, the chief and elders of the community organized a grand farewell durbar in my honour. I preached to the entire community at the durbar and prayed for them all.

The next morning, the chief, the elders, and almost the entire community walked me for 5 miles to the village where I could get a vehicle, as they saw me off. It was very emotional. The chief and all the people where in tears as the "boneshaker" (a wooden framed car) I boarded took off. I have since visited the village again only on three occasions.

5

ONE YEAR KINGDOM SERVICE

ONE YEAR KINGDOM SERVICE BEFORE UNIVERSITY

After my national service, I had no desire of entering the university for two reasons:

1. I was not admitted for the course (Land Economy) I had chosen at University of Science and Technology. I was rather offered a course I had no interest in.

2. I had received few prophetic confirmations on the call of God on my life, and as such, I did not want to go to the university any longer.

I finally made up my mind to give up university for ministry. I was assured of a scholarship for Idahosa Bible School in Nigeria. Whilst waiting for the green light to go to the Idahosa Bible School, I got fully engaged in ministry work, particularly in town fellowship activities.

A group of elderly Full Gospel Businessmen Fellowship members sat me down and admonished me to give up my dream of going to Bible school and rather go to the university. To them, I was still young and could easily go to the Bible School after my university education. I listened to their counsel and decided to go to the university. Unfortunately, it was too late for me to enter the university that year.

I decided to offer that whole year for Kingdom Service. I also made up my mind to go to university of Ghana rather than University of Science and Technology. I used the opportunity to improve my grades by re-writing one of the subjects I offered in my A Level examination.

I stayed at home that whole year fully sold out to the work of the ministry in towns and schools.

During this one year of Kingdom Service, I was voted the Akwatia Christian Fellowship (The Town Fellowship - S.U) President. The town fellowships were the Scripture Union Groups in the various towns. Membership was often made up of matured working brethren who had passed through scripture union in their school days, Scripture Union students on vacation or awaiting to further their education, and persons won to Christ through the group's outreach and evangelistic activities. I was the youngest person ever to be made president of a Town Fellowship, presiding over adult brethren.

I was also appointed the Scripture Union District President by virtue of my position as the president of the Akwatia Christian Fellowship to oversee; Akwatia, Kade, Asamankese and Akyim Oda fellowships.

IMPACTS DURING MY TOWN FELLOWSHIP LEADERSHIP

During this period, I led the fellowship into several daytime prayers in the bush.

We engaged in several open-air crusades.

We pursued the reformation and full establishment of both Osenase and Toperamang fellowships. We travelled to have fellowship with them frequently.

I visited, organized programs, and preached at all the major towns under my District.

My ministry became very known in Kade, Asamankese, Akyim-Oda, Akyim Swedru and Akyim Awisa.

Aside, the town fellowships, different churches as well as full gospel businessmen fellowships in all these towns invited me for programs.

I also got involved in Assemblies of God church which had just began in the town. I could however not be actively involved in the activities of the church due to my engagements in the fellowship work and travels.

SOME INITIATIVES DURING THIS ERA

I came up with a few Kingdom Initiatives during this period.

I got a megaphone and a team of brothers with whom I went for dawn broadcasting.

I went with a team of brothers on Market days to some of the big towns just to preach and share gospel tracts.

I rode a bicycle one Sunday to a small farming village of about 20 miles from where I was, to preach to the chief of the village and his household. They accepted the Lord and welcomed me to come and start a church in the village. Today, there is a vibrant church in that community under the supervision of one of my converts. Through that initiative, we built a community school and took some secondary school graduates (who could no longer further their education) from a nearby town to teach as "pupil teachers" (untrained teachers). The school was later taken over by the Ghana Education Service.

I used to go to the house of the Chief Administrator of the Mines Hospital in Akwatia occasionally to pray with her family. As a result of this I found favour with her and got her approval to conduct church services every Sunday morning for the patients at the Hospital. These services were held at the out-patient department of the Hospital (OPD). I got a friend to assist me in this task. This friend is now a pastor in Koforidua. The hospital church service was so refreshing. We went from ward to ward to pray for patients who were unable to attend the OPD service due to their condition.

I also visited the St. Dominic Hospital (the main hospital in Akwatia) every other Sunday in the afternoon to preach and pray for the sick.

Through my relationship with the Principal of the Akwatia Technical Institute, I was often invited to preach to the entire school on Sunday evenings.

I held a lot of programs in the following secondary schools during this period: Asuom Secondary School, Asamankese Secondary School, Joe Oduro School, Oda, and Akim Swedru Secondary School.

6

UNIVERSITY DAYS MINISTRY

MINISTRY ON LEGON CAMPUS

E ven before I entered the university, I used to be invited for programs as a preacher at the Legon (University of Ghana) and UCC (University of Cape Coast) campuses. This was during my one year stay at home.

I was therefore familiar with ministry work on the campus terrain. However, during the first semester of my first year at Legon, I was virtually absent from campus every weekend. My travelling ministry had fast begun to grow during my stay at home. I had programs fixed for almost every weekend which always took me somewhere outside campus every weekend.

However, by the second semester of my first year on campus, I had made up my mind to settle down and be fully involved in campus ministry. I joined Ghafes (Ghana Fellowship of Evangelical Students). I became actively involved in the school outreach ministry of Ghafes. I also joined the Assemblies of God Campus Ministry (AGCM). In my second year, both Ghafes and AGCM approached me for leadership positions. I gave up on Ghafes and became the President of AGCM (Assemblies of God Campus Ministry). I however remained actively involved in Ghafes throughout my university days.

SOME MINISTRY IMPACTS ON CAMPUS

My ministry became known and accepted on Legon Campus. I preached severally on the Ghafes (Ghana Fellowship of Evangelical Students) platform. I also preached in most of the denominations on campus:

Pensa (Pentecost Students Association), Anglican, MPU (Methodist Presbyterian Union) and Baptist. As for the AGCM, I became more like a full-time pastor. Some of the lecturers who attended services with us like Prof Nabila and Prof Oduro Afriyie addressed me as their pastor.

Members of AGCM and other denominations commended me to their home churches. As a result, I had more preaching invitations than I could honour whilst a student on campus. I tried to fix most of these invitations in the vacation periods to enable me honour them.

MINISTRY INITIATIVES & OUTREACHES AT LEGON

1. Together with my leadership team, AGCM acquired a new enthusiasm and zeal for vacation missions.

2. Through the visionary dream of our leadership team, AGCM bought a bus for our vacation missions and outreaches.

3. I never gave up my involvement in Ghafes, though burdened with the task of leading AGCM. I was part of the remarkable Ghafes outreach to communities in Afram plains during the university lockdown period between 1995 & 1996. We held crusades and door to door evangelism throughout the communities on the plains.

4. Under my leadership, AGCM & PENSA teamed up to organize a big crusade at Amasaman to win souls for the Assemblies of God church that had just started. I preached powerfully that day, and people run out of their bedrooms in their night wears to surrender their lives to the Lord.

5. I was also able to call on Ghafes to team up with AGCM to organize a 3-day crusade at Kissema (a suburb of Achimota) to win souls for the Assemblies

of God church that had just started there. Kissema being close to Legon, some of the AGCM members were tasked to help them in the following up of the souls and help the new church on Sundays.

6. Legon campus was simply the apex grounds for my ministry. I was travelling out of Legon to preach at UCC (University of Cape Coast), IPS (Institute of Professional Studies – now University of Professional Studies), PTC (Presbyterian Training College), Kyebi Training College, Komenda Training College, Korle-bu Medical School etc.

7

DAYS OF ITINERARY MINISTRY

MINISTRY AFTER UNIVERSITY EDUCATION

I found myself back in the university (Legon) environment for one whole year after my university education. Although I chose Wa (the capital of Upper West Region) for my national service, I was among the few students called back to do our national service on campus. I was specifically assigned to the office of Professor George Benneh at the Population Impact Project at the Geography Department. Prof. Benneh had just finished serving as the VC -Vice Chancellor of the university. The university usually take note of students who are called back to serve on campus, since such students are usually seen as potential lecturers and given some encouragement by some lecturers in that regard.

Almost every evening during my national service on Legon campus, I had to preach at a program outside campus. It was incredibly stressful. After, the duration of my national service, I gave up the dream of becoming a lecturer. My professors were highly disappointed in me, but I knew I just did the right thing. I left campus just to focus on ministry.

Whilst doing my national service, my friend Harold Afflu (now a pastor at Ipswich, UK) and myself formed a para church movement known as MISSIONS & PRAYER NETWORK. A few of our Legon mates and friends joined us and we were doing great. We initiated few internal mission outreaches which were successful. Once my national service was over, I focused on the Missions and Prayer Network whilst embarking on ministry as an itinerary preacher all over the country.

Missions & Prayer Network was registered and I secured an enviable office for it. My friend Harold left for the UK and wrote to inform me to go all out alone with the dream since he was not coming back to live in Ghana. A few of the committed brethren also travelled out of the country to further their education whilst others got employed in jobs that took them out of Accra.

I therefore made up my mind to rather focus on my denomination—Assemblies of God even though I maintained and operated from the Missions & Prayer Network Office.

I applied for a Master's program in theological studies in an Assemblies of God Theological College in the UK. My Spiritual Father the Rev. (now Rtd) Alex Ofori Amankwa endorsed my forms for me and I was admitted.

I immediately travelled to attend the school in the United Kingdom. On my return I was commissioned as a full-fledged Evangelist in Assemblies of God. I had invitations for crusades, revival services, youth camps, women ministry camps, men ministry camps and many more platforms even outside the Assemblies of God circles.

Whilst, engaged in ministry as an itinerary preacher with zeal, the Lord put on my heart to secure a vast tract of land and set up an Assemblies of God Prayer Retreat Centre. By the Grace of God, the Fresh Grace Prayer Ground was opened and dedicated by the Rev. Alex Ofori Amankwaa on December 31, 2010. The centre which is situated at Brekumanso near Asamankese in the Eastern Region provides a conducive environment for persons who wish to retreat and spend some time in prayer. The General Superintendent the Rev. Prof. Paul Frimpong Manso and the General Treasurer, the Rev. Dr. Ato Bentil have both visited the centre. Several programmes are organised at the centre throughout the year ranging from prayer meetings, retreats and training sessions for Ministers of Assemblies of God, in the Eastern Region B.

During my itinerary ministry, the Rev. Alex Ofori Amankwa advised me to enroll in the Assemblies of God Bible School in Saltpond for the diploma in theology though I had jumped ahead of it for a master's in theology. I willingly obeyed and I am grateful to him for his counsel. The basics I learnt at Saltpond have indeed improved my delivery and made me more acceptable in most Assemblies of God churches. Until then, many pastors did not know I had had training from an Assemblies of God Seminary in the UK.

When Eastern Region B was calved out of the Assemblies of God, Eastern Region, the Regional Superintendent, the late Rev. David Frimpong Boateng appointed me as the Regional Prayer Director. I was to form a strong Regional prayer team made up of two prayer warriors from each local assembly. I was to map out prayer retreats and conferences for the region and organise annual pastor's prayer retreats and annual pastors' wives' prayer retreats in collaboration with the Regional Superintendent. I was also tasked to oversee a special Regional Holy Ghost Baptism and Deliverance prayer meetings at the Prayer center every year.

I had barely started this huge assignment alongside my itinerary ministry and my ministry at the Fresh Grace Prayer Ground when the General Superintendent of Assemblies of God, Ghana – Rev. Prof. Paul Frimpong Manso assigned me to Canada as an interim pastor for the Lighthouse Assembly of God church in Toronto.

8

INTERNATIONAL MISSION

MINISTRY IN CANADA

I left Ghana in January 2016 for this new assignment in Canada which was to last for a period of 6 months.

I took over the church in Canada on Sunday January 29, 2016 as an interim Pastor. My task was to stabilize the church, teach and prepare the grounds for the coming in of a substantive Pastor.

I was however asked to continue with my task as interim Pastor after the 6months period had expired.

I was eventually asked by the General Superintendent to be the substantive Pastor of the church for a duration of two years. He personally travelled from Accra to Toronto to officially induct me as the substantive Pastor of Lighthouse Assemblies of God church in May 2017.

After the 2-year duration, my assignment was extended yet again for 2 more years which has just expired, now I await further directions as to the next move of God in my life.

SOME MAJOR MINISTRY INITIATIVES AT LIGHTHOUSE

1. The first initiative I brought on board was the indoor salvation and healing crusade.

2. I also brought on board the Annual Street Feeding Project where we all go to town on the last Saturday of our Breakthrough Conference to share food to street dwellers.

3. I introduced the all-groups meeting on every first Saturday of the month. This was welcomed and embraced by all, sparking up a new fire in our group meetings. Families drive to church together and then go into their various groups: Men, Women, Joy and Youth.

4. I took the YOUTH, the WOMEN, and the MEN for a 3-day Camp separately at different times of the year. The peculiarity of these camp meetings was that I went with each group and taught them throughout the duration. I engaged them in at least 5 -7 speaking and praying sessions. We left on Friday evening and returned on Sunday morning straight to church. Hitherto they had camps, some of them joint, with diverse speakers and outlines.

5. We had several revival programs with diverse captions like JESUS CONVENTION, KRUPTOS CAMPAIGN, DEEPER ROOTS RETREAT etc.

6. I also introduced the Annual Couples Weekend Retreat. This was either scheduled for before Easter or in the 2nd Quarter of the year. We would normally start on Friday night with the speaker sharing a message on Family Life. The whole of Saturday devoted to couples with the speaker or speakers sharing messages on marital issues. The program would end with Sunday church service with the speaker sharing a message on family life.

7. I initiated an annual awards day which had a committee in charge. This was extraordinarily successful.

8. I established the PSM (Practical School of Ministry) class to instruct those with potentials in ministry.

9. I appointed two church members as lay pastors. Pastor Ben Asante-Yerenkyi as my Senior Assistant Pastor and Pastor George Agyeman also an Assistant Pastor, next to Pastor Ben.

10. I appointed three Prayer Ministers who lead most of the prayer sessions in the church. They are Minister Ernest Boateng, Minister Kofi Essuman and Minister Charles Baah. I identified these Ministers as potential persons for ministry if given space and some training.

The impact of my ministry work in Canada, is best chronicled in the form of text messages I have received over the period from some of the members on how my ministry has blessed them. I share some of these messages of the members leaving out their names:

A MEMBER

When my dear husband passed away almost two years ago, that was the lowest point in my life. I had nobody to cry to and yes, I had family, but I needed someone more than that. I didn't really have a stable church at that moment but when I cried to Pastor

Boniface, he not only comforted me with the word of God, Pastor came home to pray with me and gave me direction and told me that everything was going to be alright. He planted me into the Church family and gave me roots to stand still. I owe a lot to Pastor Boniface he is truly a man of God and he is ever ready to help his family of God. I want to say Pastor God bless you and God restore all you lost to make the Church family happy and may God open doors that will bring blessings to you and the entire Church. Thank you for being a good pastor to me.

A MEMBER

Good morning Pastor. Your ministry has really impacted my life since you have been here. I now understand the scriptures better and I can preach it to others. Your preaching has also made me a better person. It has given me a better outlook on life. Thank you very much.

A MEMBER

Since I joined the church two years ago, your teaching has helped me to grow spiritually. Your preaching has been of tremendous help to my life. And for that I say a big thank you.

God bless you and your family.

A MEMBER

Hi Pastor, your preaching gives me a lot of wisdom. Thank you very much!

A MEMBER

Good morning Pastor! Just want to say thank you for welcoming me back to the Assembly of God family and the support you provided me and Kofi during our traditional marriage.

A MEMBER

Good morning Pastor. Thanks for giving us the opportunity to hear the sermon via WhatsApp because for me I miss church every other Sunday due to work. I also love the practicality of how you relate and present the sermon. I can comprehend well in relation to what the bible requires of me. Your preaching and teaching is much appreciated and valued.

A MEMBER

Pastor, your preaching and teachings inspired me to become a member of Lighthouse Assembly of God. Thank you, Papa!

A MEMBER

Thanks so much for your love to inspire me to become a better Christian.

A MEMBER

My dear Pastor,

I am saying again what I have always been saying about you, and everyone in the Church can testify:

1. The Church was near collapse when you took over. Our Sunday service attendance at that time did not even march our Friday Evening service now.

2. Your sacrifice...leaving your wife far behind. I cannot do that. I went through it once in UK for a year and I vowed never to do it again. Very tempting...but you are enduring.

3. As you know I have been sending your messages across the world and for me personally...I know I am

much better off in my understanding of the Word and in Prayer...

4. I can go on and on. You have done very well.

5. If you **must go** at the end of the five years…then we must pray hard for another person like you...

A MEMBER

Good morning Pastor. How are you doing this morning. I hope you are doing great. Thank you very much and God bless you and keep you always. I have been blessed with your ministry. I can see that you are good to me because since I came to Lighthouse, I have seen things change in my life. Thank you very much.

God bless you.

A MEMBER

Hello Pastor, I really admire your courage in delivering the gospel. More than several occasions you have preached on issues I was/have been grappling with (sometimes, the night before the Sunday I might be wrestling with a spiritual question and then you will deliver right to the core of it on the Sunday. I remember texting you and saying that I do not cherish unwarranted persecution, not understanding the works of the spirit, as you discussed in your 'spiritus class'.

Simply said, God has used you as a vessel to communicate with me, specifically on several occasions. My growth is being harnessed and I thank you for being a conduit!

Blessings!

A MEMBER

Good morning Rev. I trust you had a good rest. Congratulations again on completing four years at Lighthouse.

I know I just joined the ministry. I have been greatly impacted by your teachings and leadership. You are a man of wisdom and I am happy to learn from you at this point in my life. As God directs you, wherever you feel I could serve am willing.

God bless you.

A MEMBER

Hi Pastor, I hope you doing great by God's grace.

You are a great Pastor, thank you for the sermons you preach and the prayers you lift for us. Thank you for the sacrifice and service. Indeed, you are a great Pastor. Your hard work and sacrifices are appreciated. God richly bless you with more grace and oil.

A MEMBER

My Bishop God bless you richly for your wonderful work you are doing which has made me and some friends understand the word of God through your preaching. I always share your messages to my family and friends all over. Any time I do not send to them they call and ask for it. I have a cousin in Germany whom your preaching has made great impact in her life and she always wants to listen to you. Me and my family really appreciate the changes your messages have bless us with. If I continue talking, I will talk till tomorrow. Thank you and God bless you and increase your ministry with more anointing.

A MEMBER

Your presence has made me self-conscious of the importance of prayer. I meditate more often throughout the day. God bless you for your influence.

A MEMBER

Pastor,

I thank God for Lady Evelyn. I thank God for your life. God bless you for being the Pastor of the Lighthouse Assembly of God.

I congratulate you for chalking 4 years with the church! I appreciate your ministry. However, as a human being, we all have lapses. We falter here and there.

It is my ardent prayer that, you will spend many more years with us and even be a permanent pastor for us.

Your messages, no matter how bitter they are, are what we need at this end time. God richly bless you for coming to Canada to be our pastor.

A MEMBER

Hello Pastor, you have really been a tremendous blessing to me throughout your years of service!! I have really grown in the knowledge of the WORD of God, and I have really become eternity conscious day by day. Thank you! May God bless you and continue to use you to change lives.

A MEMBER

Happy Fourth Anniversary Pastor. On this day I thank God for your Life. Had it not been the regular and frequent church programs you organize which I am always privileged to attend I would have gone down into very deep depression state.

Your regular programs and sermons over these four years always take my mind off stress related issues and it gives me hope.

Church and its related activities have contributed immensely to my inner joy and peace so far.

A MEMBER

Pastor,

Your presence with me over the past 4years has helped me in my prayer life, understanding the word of God and the true essence of Christianity.

A MEMBER

Pastor Boniface I like Your Ministry Especially Friday Prayer Meeting

I love it.

God bless U for the good job.

A MEMBER

Dear Pastor, thank you for all the teachings that you give us daily, I want to say I am always touched and poised to live right before God. God bless you and give you each day a word for us. We love you.

A MEMBER

Hello Pastor,

I was a bit sad when you kind of announced that you may not be here with us after some time.

One of the days I was instantly transformed by God's word shared on a Wednesday (last year) You were teaching us about the End time: The Rapture, The Marriage Supper, The Tribulation, The Millennium, etc. I wish this could be preached all over again on Sundays.

God be with you.

A MEMBER

Hello Pastor Boniface, Vic and I just want to congratulate you on your four years as pastor of Lighthouse. And we wish to let you know that when Vic and I started looking for a church, we were not sure Lighthouse will be the church for us until I heard you preach. Please do not misunderstand me. We love how the whole congregation have been so welcoming, but we stayed mostly because of you and I think you should know that. So may God richly bless and protect you.

A MEMBER

Thank you, my Pastor, for your preaching and teaching. Yeah! your preaching encourages me to come to church every Friday. I always encourage myself to come because of you. Thank God for your life Pastor Boniface.

A MEMBER

Hi pastor, thank you for being such a great preacher.

Your preaching has made me a better person.

I pray that God will continue to bless you with more wisdom to touch more souls if you live in Jesus Name.

A MEMBER

Hi Pastor, ever since you came to Lighthouse I have learned to appreciate listening to the word because you communicate your preaching's in a way that I can understand.

A MEMBER

Hello Daddy, Thank you very much for your teachings. It has changed my mind towards life and my Christian journey. Your recent teachings on prayer have really helped me and showed me how I can handle situations. It has brought peace in my family. Thank You Daddy. God bless you.

A MEMBER

My prayer life has really improved through your ministry.

Thank you pastor.

God bless you.

A MEMBER

Dear Pastor, I have not been in the church for long, but I have been blessed by your teachings on salvation and I am assured that I will make heaven by the grace of God if I strive harder and obey all your directions. Am blessed to be a member of your church. Happy 4th anniversary Sir. God bless you.

A MEMBER

Dear Pastor, in the past two years I have been in the church you have been a father figure to me. And, I have become a great mother and a wife because of your teaching in church. The salvation studies you have been giving us has opened my eyes and I am careful how I live my life because one day I will die, and God is going to judge me.

Pastor Boniface I thank God for being my pastor.

A MEMBER

Pastor, I am extremely blessed to have you as my pastor. Your style of preaching has a strong impact on my understanding. May the Almighty God richly you and all your entire family.

A MEMBER

Good evening Pastor. I would just like to say that prior to you coming to Lighthouse, I felt like I had plateaued or become stagnant in my walk with Christ, so much so, that I did not even feel like coming to church anymore but the way you preach the Word and teach through Scripture is something that I thank God for. I am also grateful that when I had backslid and approached you, you did not treat me with contempt or judge me but instead prayed for me. I am grateful Pastor Boniface. God Bless you!

A MEMBER

Man of God you are a good Pastor.

Because of your preaching, that is why every Sunday I come to church.

A MEMBER

Hi Pastor believe me; you have been a big blessing to have as our pastor in the Lighthouse family. Daddy, one thing I love about your message in church is that most of the time when you are preaching it seems like you are living with me or someone have talked about me to you. This is how powerful your messages are.

A MEMBER

My papa, please I must confess that since you came to Lighthouse your ministry has made a great impact on my life. Again, papa thank you for allowing us to be part of your ministry. God richly bless you.

A MEMBER

Reverend, you have been a blessing to me and my husband. Your Ministry has made a lot of difference in our lives since you became our leader and pastor. May God continue to bless you, and may you continue to be a blessing to us always. Much Love.

A MEMBER

Good evening Papa.

God bless you for the great impact you have made in my life and my family. It is hard to have kingdom minded ministers like your kind especially in this end time and we count ourselves most blessed to be under your ministry. Thank you very much.

A MEMBER

Hello papa, thank you for opening my eyes more about salvation. God bless you.

A MEMBER

Good afternoon Reverend: Last year your teachings about Salvation caused me to take a particularly good look at my personal walk with Christ and make some changes. Thank You!

A MEMBER

Dear Papa, Alb and I have had deep meaningful discussions after listening to you ministering the word which has resulted in increased understanding of the bible. Through God ministering through you to us we have been on the road of great discovery having been pleasantly surprised so many times on secrets and deep knowledge gained from bible verses we sometimes have come across in the past but meant nothing to us. From "Ho such a man" to Kruptos Dominos we have been enriched with information that is amazing. We also do not forget and are able to share due to your down to earth practical interpretation you receive from the Lord Almighty. Your "unplanned" evening prayer meetings, a direction I honestly believe you receive from the Holy Spirit always occur when we, the church, need to fire up our prayer life. Thank you for being willing to be used by God to lift us up when we are running low on spiritual fuel. Through the emphasis to pray you have instituted from God's direction we are learning to reach to God as individuals and us a church. Thank you very much Papa. God richly bless you and always top you up.

A MEMBER

Good morning Pastor. Since you have been here, my understanding of the bible has changed. I understand the word much better than before. I like how you break down the points for better understanding. May God continue to give you wisdom.

A MEMBER

Good evening Reverend. Friday prayer meetings are particularly good to me and the preaching is powerful. God bless your Sir. Thank you for leading and inspiring us to pray well.

A MEMBER

Good evening Reverend, please this is Bee. I have been in the church for a short time, but you have touched and blessed me very much by way of your preaching. You teach salvation and kingdom messages. I have not had the chance to attend weekly meetings which I am working on but with the Sunday services, they always inspire me, and you have been a blessing to me because I love to come listen to the unadulterated word of God you preach.

A MEMBER

Good evening oooo Paapa,

I just want to appreciate your time with us till date. You have contributed greatly to my family especially for my husband to be back to church. The message on life after death has brought great awareness to me. (It is not about somebody but me).

Thank you greatly and God richly bless you.

A MEMBER

Thank you, Pastor Boniface, for teaching and training us to live in Victory for Christ. May Our Lord add more years to your life.

I have also seen a remarkable improvement in Men ministry since you took over.

God richly bless you.

A MEMBER

Bishop I salute you!

Amongst everything else, for the lay appointments today, I know God is truly at work!

A MEMBER

Good evening Osofo (Pastor), myself and my husband want to thank you for helping us to gain more knowledge and understanding about the word of God. All the preaching and teachings have changed us in diverse ways. We pray that your word will continue to impact lives. If anyone has been really blessed by your teachings and sermons, it is me and my family.

God richly blessed you Pastor.

A MEMBER

Reverend, you have been a blessing to my life since you took over our church. Your teachings have made me come out from doing bad things drinking alcohol going to strip joint etc. Thanks!

A MEMBER

Dear Pastor, your coming to Lighthouse, have made me more interested in going deeper in the things of God. Deeper in my personal prayer and devotional life, and not just doing things out of obligation and duty (which is an easy trap to fall into) but doing it from my heart.

One thing I will never forget was when you spoke a blessing over the church, and it was recorded, and you sent it to us. There was a night when I woke up suddenly and it felt like a dark presence was in the room. So, I started speaking in tongues. And I felt like the Holy Spirit told me to play that prayer. After it finished playing, I felt peace in the room, and I was able to sleep.

Your teachings really do impact me. There is always something that you say that will replay in my mind over and over. For example, you once told us not to let depression take over us. And before that, I would go through many episodes of depression for unknown reasons (which is why you probably saw a change in me at a certain point). At first, it seemed so easy to become depressed that I did not understand how you can just not allow it to take over. But after allowing the Holy Spirit to help me understand, I realized that it is a mindset. That as a man thinks, so is he. So, from then, I changed my thinking concerning depression and those episodes stopped. I would not allow it anymore. So, I thank you for that.

I also remember speaking to you before I entered university and was telling you about how I did not know what program I should do, and you told me to do what my parents said I should do. And I did not understand why at first, but I did it, and I ended up loving the program I am in.

Some programs/series/teachings that I will never forget:

- Deeper Roots!!!!!!!

- Kruptos Campaign

- The Prayer Summit we just finished (which was much needed)

- First Love (Wednesday Bible Studies Series)

• Last year's Breakthrough Conference dramatically changed my outlook and my thinking

• Your teachings on the rapture. You impact me more than I show. And even though I might not understand what you say or do at times, I know that you carry wisdom. Thank you for being my Pastor. You have shown to be everything I prayed for before you came to Lighthouse. Love you!

A MEMBER

Good morning Pastor, you have been a great blessing to me since coming to Lighthouse. Your teachings have transformed all areas of my life: marriage, job, parenting, friendship etc. They have also transformed my spiritual life. Before you came my spiritual life consisted of coming to church only on Sundays and little prayer here and there, with no assurance of salvation. But now I am in a totally different place since getting saved and baptized by you in 2017 followed by Holy Spirit baptism in 2018. Christ has set my mind at peace. I love him and cannot seem to get enough of his word. This hunger for more of his Word is overwhelming at times. I pray God will continue to bless your Ministry.

A MEMBER

Reverend, I just want to tell you that you have impacted my life since I rejoined this church. You have taught me how to understand the Bible content and how to interpret the bible right.

I need more.

Thank you so much.

God bless you for your efforts and help.

Stay bless!

A MEMBER

Thanks be to the Lord for giving Pastor Boniface to Lighthouse Assembly of God. He is simply a Shepherd after your own heart.

Thank you Pastor Boniface for your rich teaching and preaching. Under your ministry, I have learned so much about the principles of the Kingdom. If I do not go to Heaven, you will certainly not be blamed at all. God richly bless you and provide for you all your heart's desire according to His will.

Have a wonderful Day!

9

PURE RELIGION

Pure religion and undefiled before God and the Father is this, To visit the fatherless and widows in their affliction, and to keep himself unspotted from the world.—James 1:27 KJV

The Bible text above explains that among the characteristics considered as pure religion before God is to be able to assist in your own small way.

By the grace of God, my wife and I have been of some support to people in the ministry by way of assistance such as, sponsoring some people through Bible school, giving out car donation to one or two persons, and financial assistance in some instances.

We have also supported five rural churches to acquire plots of land and have supported some rural churches to put up church buildings and mission houses.

We have on our own built 3 church buildings for 3 rural churches.

We also on our own acquired the vast tract of land for the Fresh Grace Prayer Retreat Center.

We contributed more than 70 percent towards the putting up of all the structures and works on the Fresh Grace Prayer Retreat Center.

For more than a decade, my wife and I with the assistance of some good people, have been making donations in the form of provisions and money to more than 150 needy widows every year at Christmas to the tune of thousands of dollars.

10

CHRONICLES OF MINISTRY WORK

THE 'PINK SHEET COLLATION' OF MY MINISTRY

Acommon phrase in Ghana after election is the collation of pink sheets. The election results are often tabulated on a pink sheet hence the phrase. In this chapter, I wish to chronicle some of the ministry works I have done over the years. Apart from assisting to plant and a build some rural churches, my work and ministry over the years could be best be chronicled as follows:

To the glory of God, the following are places where I have held crusades in my work and Ministry in Ghana:

1. GCD AMANFROM CRUSADE
2. GCD QUARTERS CRUSADE
3. AKWATIA TOWNSHIP CRUSADE
4. BOADUA TOWNSHIP CRUSADE
5. TOPREMANG TOWNSHIP CRUSADE
6. KADE TOWNSHIP CRUSADE
7. AWISA TOWNSHIP CRUSADE
8. AKIM SWEDRU TOWNSHIP CRUSADE
9. AKYIM-ODA TOWNSHIP CRUSADE
10. AKYIM GYADEM CRUSADE
11. AKYIM – MANSO CRUSADE
12. ASAMANKESE TOWNSHIP CRUSADE
13. OWURAM VILLAGE CRUSADE
14. BREKUMANSO VILLAGE CRUSADE
15. YAW TANO VILLAGE CRUSADE
16. KOFI PARE VILLAGE CRUSADE
17. ESAASE VILLAGE CRUSADE

18. AKANTENG VILLAGE CRUSADE
19. AYEKOKYE TOWNSHIP CRUSADE
20. ASUOKWO TOWNSHIP CRUSADE
21. ADEISO TOWNSHIP CRUSADE
22. NSAWAM TOWNSHIP CRUSADE
23. ADOAGYIRI TOWNSHIP CRUSADE
24. AMASAMAN TOWNSHIP CRUSADE
25. ACHIMOTA KISSEMAN CRUSADE
26. DWORWULU TOWNSHIP CRUSADE
27. PIG FARM TOWNSHIP CRUSADE
28. KWASHIMAN TOWNSHIP CRUSADE
29. AUNTIE AKU- SANTA MARIA CRUSADE
30. ANYAA TOWNSHIP CRUSADE
31. MANGOASE – ACCRA CRUSADE
32. DANSOMAN MPOASE CRUSADE
33. SAKUMONO VILLAGE CRUSADE
34. SPINTEX ROAD CRUSADE
35. TESHIE - NUNGUA CRUSADE
36. AKUSE TOWNSHIP CRUSADE
37. MAAFI KUMASI TOWNSHIP CRUSADE

38. SUGAKOPE TOWNSHIP CRUSADE
39. ADIDOME TOWNSHIP CRUSADE
40. KOFORIDUA AYIGBETOWN CRUSADE
41. EFFIDUASE TOWNSHIP CRUSADE
42. KUKURANTUMI TOWNSHIP CRUSADE
43. AKYIM NEW-TAFO CRUSADE
44. AKYIM OLD-TAFO CRUSADE
45. AKIM MAASE TOWNSHIP CRUSADE
46. BUNSO TOWNSHIP CRUSADE
47. AKIM-ANKAASE TOWNSHIP CRUSADE
48. ASAMAN TAMFOE CRUSADE
49. AKYIM ANYINAM CRUSADE
50. AKYIM OSENO TOWNSHIP CRUSADE
51. AKYIM KWABENG CRUSADE
52. AKIM MMOSO VILLAGE CRUSADE
53. AKIM ABOMOSO TOWNSHIP CRUSADE
54. AKIM ASUOM TOWNSHIP CRUSADE
55. DONKOKROM TOWNSHIP CRUSADE
56. MAAME KROBO TOWNSHIP CRUSADE
57. CAPE COAST TOWNSHIP CRUSADE

58. PRESTEA TOWNSHIP CRUSADE
59. DUNKWA OFFIN TOWNSHIP CRUSADE
60. BOGOSO TOWNSHIP CRUSADE
61. AKYIM ASUBOA TOWN CRUSADE
62. CHAIREE VILLAGE CRUSADE
63. KUZIE VILLAGE CRUSADE
64. BOLGATANGA TOWNSHIP CRUSADE
65. OSENASE TOWNSHIP CRUSADE
66. ASUBONI TOWNSHIP CRUSADE
67. ODA-NKWATA TOWNSHIP CRUSADE
68. NSUTAM TOWNSHIP CRUSADE
69. ABERMU TOWNSHIP CRUSADE
70. GONGO VILLAGE CRUSADE

By the Grace of God, the following are some of the Schools & Colleges in Ghana I have preached in over the years:

1. AKWATIA TECHNICAL INSTITUTE
2. ASUOM SECONDARY
3. ASAMANKESE SECONDARY
4. ODA SECONDARY
5. AKIM SWEDRU SECONDARY
6. SAINT THOMAS SECONDARY
7. JOE ODURO SCHOOL
8. NEW JUABEN SECONDARY
9. OKUAPEMAN SECONDARY
10. ADONTENG SECONDARY
11. ABURI GIRLS
12. PRESBYTERIAN TRAINING COLLEGE, AKROPONG
13. KYEBI TRAINING COLLEGE
14. MOUNT MARY TRAINING COLLEGE, SOMANYA
15. HO UNIVERSITY OF ALLIED SCIENCES

16. ASUOGYAMAN SECONDARY
17. AMESS (AKIM OLD TAFO)
18. KOMENDA TRAINING COLLEGE
19. UNIVERSITY OF CAPE COAST
20. UNIVERSITY OF MINES, TARKWA
21. UNIVERSITY OF EDUCATION, WINNEBA
22. UNIVERSITY OF EDUCATION, KUMASI
23. UNIVERSITY OF SCIENCE AND TECHNOLOGY
24. SUNYANI POLYTENIC
25. KUMASI POLYTECHNIC
26. UNIVERSITY OF DEVELOPMENT, NYANKPALA
27. MEDICAL SCHOOL KORLEBU
28. AKYIM WENCHI SALVATION ARMY SECONDARY
29. KOFORIDUA POLYTECHNIC
30. LIBERTY SPECIALIST SCHOOL

These are some of the Towns and villages I have preached in:

1. AKWATIA
2. BOADUA
3. KADE
4. ASUBONI
5. BAMENASE
6. AKWATIA NO. 4
7. SWABEH
8. OKUMANI
9. AWEASO
10. NEW ABIREM
11. AFOSU
12. GYADEM
13. ODA-NKWATA
14. AKYIM WENCHI
15. KWAE
16. ABOMOSO
17. KWAABENG
18. ANYINAM

19. AKIM SWEDRU
20. AKYIM ODA
21. AKYIM AWISA
22. WINNEBA
23. AKIM AKROSO
24. ASAMANKESE
25. OSENASE
26. TOPREMANG
27. BREKUMANSO
28. OWURAM
29. PABI
30. KOFI PARE
31. ASUOKUO
32. APUNAPU
33. KYEBI
34. BONSO
35. NSUTAM
36. AKYIM ASENE
37. AKIM MANSO
38. AGONA SWREDRU

39. COUNTLESS TOWNS IN ACCRA
40. MANY PLACES IN KUMASI
41. NSAWAM
42. ADEISO
43. ADOAGYIRI
44. ABURI
45. NSAWAM PRISONS
46. CAPE COAST
47. ELIMINA
48. KOMENDA
49. TAKORADI
50. SEKONDI
51. TARKWA
52. BOGOSO
53. PRESTEA
54. DUNKWA OFFIN
55. OBUASI
56. AKOKEREE
57. SOKAGOPE
58. TEMA

59. KPONG

60. AKUSE

61. ATEMPOKU

62. HOHOE

63. HO

64. DZODZE

65. AFLAO

66. KETA

67. ODUMASE

68. AGORMANYA-ABLOTSI

69. SOMANYA

70. ADUKRUM

71. AKROPONG

72. KUKRANTUMI

73. ASOKOREE

74. NEW TAFO

75. OLD TAFO

76. MAASE

77. BEGORO

78. KONONGO

79. EJISU
80. MIM
81. GOASO
82. KENYAASE
83. SUNYANI
84. TAKYIMAN
85. WÈNCHI
86. NEW DROBO
87. BREKUM
88. TAMALE
89. NYANPALA
90. BOLGATANGA
91. BOTANGA
92. BAWKU
93. BOLE
94. WA
95. CHAIRE
96. KALEO GANKO
97. JIRAPA
98. LAWRA

99. NANDOM
100. HAMILE
101. ASSIN FOSU
102. AKOSOMBO
103. AKLOMUASE
104. NUASO
105. NKAWKAW
106. ASSIN FOSU
107. ESAAKYIRE
108. DONKOKROM
109. MPRAESO
110. ASESEWA
111. EKYE AMANFROM
112. NSUTA
113. BREMAN ASIKUMA
114. ASHAIMAN

Churches & Fellowships preached in:

1. ASSEMBLIES OF GOD
2. PRESBYTERIAN CHURCH
3. METHODIST CHURCH
4. APOSTOLIC CHURCH OF GHANA
5. ICGC – INTERNATIONAL CENTRAL GOSPEL CHURCH
6. CHURCH OF PENTECOST
7. SALVATION ARMY
8. GHANA BAPTIST
9. GLOBAL REVIVAL
10. FOUNTAIN GATE
11. EVANGELICAL PRESBYTERIAN CHURCH
12. A NUMBER OF CHARISTMATIC CHURCHES
13. SCRIPTURE UNION
14. FULL GOSPEL BUSINESSMEN FELLOWSHIP

15. WOMEN AGLOW FELLOWSHIP
16. GAFES
17. PRISONS
18. HOSPITALS
19. UNIVERSITY CHAPLAINCIES
20. WORKPLACE FELLOWSHIPS
21. COMPANIES ANNUAL THANKSGIVING SERVICES

BOOKS PUBLISHED

1. GIVING
2. GOD SPEED
3. GLOSOLALIA
4. CLASSMATES
5. BROKEN CORDS
6. THE NEXT LEVEL
7. VITALITY PILLS
8. HOW THEY DIED
9. I BOW MY KNEES
10. WHY I FEAR HELL
11. PRAYER CAPSULES
12. 40 DAYS-40 NIGHTS
13. FLEE FORNICATION
14. DON'T GO TO HELL
15. THE COUPLES DIARY
16. DIVINE CONNECTIONS
17. BEYOUND ONE TALENT
18. THE WORST EXCHANGE
19. SPIRITUAL ENERGIZERS
20. POWER TO GET WEALTH
21. THE DOUBLE PORTION

Nations I have preached in:

1. BURKINA FASO
2. TOGO
3. COTE D'VOIRE
4. ENGLAND
5. SCOTLAND
6. USA
7. CANADA
8. GUYANA

11

50/50

FIFTY LESSONS LEARNT IN MY FIFTY YEARS

Here are fifty valuable lessons I have learnt in my fifty years of life.

1. It is great to know and serve the Lord from childhood. There is no better time in serving the Lord than when you are just a child.

2. To be committed to the service of God from childhood minimises your regrets in life. Because I followed the things of God from childhood, I have no regrets of wasted life and stories of a promiscuous life.

3. The greatest gift you could ever give to your child is to introduce him or her to the word of God. I was in primary 5 when my Dad bought me a Bible. That same year I read that Bible from cover to cover twice. I would forever say the greatest gift I ever received from my Dad was that Good news Bible.

4. When you marry a helpful and a supportive spouse you enjoy your peace of mind and you prosper faster.

5. You do not have to wait to get all you need before you start your dream life. When we married, we did not have a lot of things. When we started building our first house, we did not have it all. When we started Fresh Grace, Prayer Ground we did not have everything.

6. Those who focus on money in ministry never make it but those who focus on the ministry get blessed in diverse ways.

7. Self promotion is a sign of immaturity. Anytime you must blow your own horn it simply means you are not there yet.

8. There is no dignity in borrowing, avoid it as much as possible. I learnt exceedingly early in life not to borrow. When you keep yourself out of debt, you keep yourself out of humiliation and unnecessary stress.

9. No matter how gifted you are and how blessed you are in the grace of God; you will excel and climb higher when you are adequately trained.

10. Making a U-turn no matter how late you make it is better than going on and trusting to have a favourable outcome when you know very well you missed out on the place of turning.

11. One counsel from a mentor or a spiritual father may catapult you beyond all your efforts and labour.

12. Listening to preaching and reading books are the two major ways of improving yourself in the ministry of preaching and teaching.

13. Once you build and live in your own house no matter how small it is, you set yourself up to advance faster in your financial prosperity.

14. Never consider the people you preach to as your ATM machines. God can bless you financially through strange people and by unexpected or unconventional means.

15. Respect and pay heed to the advice and counsel from godly elders who show concern and interest in your destiny and you will be forever grateful you did.

16. Never truncate your education prematurely (if you are given the opportunity) in the name of pursuing ministry. Educating yourself up to the

tertiary level gives you a level-headed approach to ministry.

17. Whenever you are confronted with two or more good choices, ask God to choose for you and you will never go wrong.

18. The dealings of God on our lives differ. Do not expect God to favour you the same way He favours your friend.

19. No matter how painful and bitter life might deal with you, never be bitter on God. Keep serving in His vineyard with joy and keep doing what you have been called to do.

20. The greatest joy and honour you can bestow on your parents is not a grand funeral on their death. The best you can do for them is to love them, visit them, provide for them, and take good care of them whilst they are alive.

21. Until you have cultivated the friendship of some poor, maimed, or vulnerable persons in this life, you can never claim to have enjoyed the best of friendship in life.

22. In all your spending, do well to spend on the poor and the needy occasionally.

23. One of your greatest lifetime dreams as a child of God must be to build God a temple no matter how small it might be.

24. Anytime God blesses you find out if someone else's blessing is in it. God blesses us so we may also be a blessing to others.

25. A pastor must be an example in all things including giving. If your financial contribution is among the least in a church you pastor, then you do not deserve to be the pastor of the church.

26. No pastor should leave the planning of his future in the hands of a church committee. Make your

own plans for your future and trust God for the unknown.

27. No one prospers in ministry on salary. We prosper in ministry by fulfilling our ministry fully.

28. Friendship is not mandatory. Choose your friends wisely and prayerfully. Everyone cannot be your friend.

29. Life is in stages. At each stage in life, you will lose some good friends and gain some good ones. The earlier you accept this reality the better.

30. Know whom you are responsible for in this life. Never allow people to force you to be responsible for them when you are not.

31. No matter how much you are liked and adored, there will always be some people who do not like or appreciate your style.

32. Do not expect God to speak to you in a dramatic form, He may not. Find out the simplest way(s) by which God speaks to you and master it.

33. The Bible is not only a book for heaven but a library for life. There are countless life lessons in all fields that one may pick up from the bible by reading and studying quite simple bible stories and texts.

34. No matter what you go through at a time, life does not pause for anybody. Learn to rise from your predicaments as fast as possible and keep marching on.

35. No one will be given the chance to come back and improve on his or her scores after death, so do your absolute best whilst you are alive.

36. Make your wife happy and you will be happy. Never treat your wife as an after thought if you desire to do well and enjoy your work or ministry.

Plan for the good of your wife and when she is happy you will enjoy your work or ministry.

37. Stop bragging about your wife and stop praising her too much on the pulpit. You may unintentionally create enemies and attacks for her.

38. Always preach the Bible and not your successes or family and you will never regret it.

39. Be careful of whom and where you share your testimony of how God has blessed you. Because your blessings when exposed to people of wrong mindset may only earn you their envy and jealousy.

40. Do your best to be nice, warm, and friendly to your in-laws always. Win their love and not their hatred.

41. Preach the word! Do not preach other ministers on the sacred pulpit of God no matter how fake

you think they are because they are not the Bible. The pulpit is for the preaching of the Bible.

42. Always travel light. Excess luggage is often a burden. Do not carry excess luggage of bitterness, unforgiveness, hatred and the likes in your journey to eternity, they will wear you off.

43. True reflection of life must always include a reflection of eternity. When this life ends, the real one begins. Never forget about this reality.

44. Honour the Lord in your giving. Never give to God as if He is a poor beggar by the traffic lights at 'Kaawokudi' junction.

45. Heaven is real, and hell is real. The greatest all time bible text of Luke 16:19-31 is not debatable.

46. Never look down on anyone because of his current situation. The outcome of his life tomorrow may put you to shame.

47. We cannot bring back the past era. When you leave an era, accept it, and embrace the new or current era. Avoid people who only appreciate and continue to live in the past era. People who do not appreciate the current might never enjoy or benefit from it.

48. No matter what you do, you cannot please everybody. Do your best and leave the rest to God.

49. Never serve the Lord or His church grudgingly. Serve God with joy and enthusiasm.

50. Life, just like a coin has two faces; one face is sweet, and the other face is bitter. You must however accept both.

ABOUT THE AUTHOR

BONIFACE DAAWIEH-KEELSON is an ordained minister of the Assemblies of God, Ghana as well as a credentialed minister with the Pentecostal Assemblies of Canada. He is a fire-brand preacher of the Gospel of Christ. Having been raised in the Lord through Scripture Union, Boniface is a very disciplined and faithful minister in the Kingdom.

He has been involved in the ministry of the Assemblies of God at a front role since his days in the university. He served as the Assemblies of God Campus Ministry President at the University of Ghana Legon in the year 1996-1997.

He is a trained minister from the Assemblies of God Theological Seminary in Ghana and the Assemblies of God Seminary in the United Kingdom.

He was commissioned an Evangelist with full ministerial rights in 2005 as an itinerant minister and a revivalist.

He established the prayer resort known as the Assemblies of God Retreat Centre [Fresh Grace Prayer Grounds] in the bushes of Brekumanso near Asamankese of the Eastern Region in Ghana.

He is currently a missionary of the Assemblies of God, Ghana to North America, and the Snr Pastor-in-charge of Lighthouse Assembly of God, Toronto, Canada.

He is married to an incredibly supportive and dynamic wife—Evelyn Ama Obenewaa Daawieh-Keelson, affectionately called Mama Evelyn by church members.

Boniface Daawieh-Keelson has won a few awards and Citations including the Global Award in Missionary Leadership (2010) from the Global Leadership Training, USA.